The Atlantic Turkey Shoot

*U-Boats off the Outer Banks
in World War II*

by
James T. Cheatham
Cmdr., USNR, Ret.

Delmar Printing Company
Charlotte, North Carolina

Front cover art
by Re Johnston

Back cover photograph
by Gan Photography

Dedicated to
Chevy,
1986-89.

Table of Contents

Illustrations

Introduction

My interest in the sea and particularly coastal North Carolina may be attributed to my family background. My mother was Louise Mann, who came from the coastal area of Hyde County and whose father, Charles Mann, carried his family each summer to Ocracoke to escape the heat, humidity and insects of the coastal region. Ocracoke is a picturesque island about thirty miles off the coast, and it makes up part of the barrier islands chain. It also lies about an equal distance from the famous Cape Hatteras and the less famous but perhaps just as important Cape Lookout.

During the pre-colonial period, Europeans found a natural harbor in the "bight" or hook of land later to be known as Cape Lookout. Here they would heave down (career) their ships for repairs and replenish their fresh water supply. During World War II, after the first months of taking tremendous ship losses, the United States Navy used this natural harbor to shield ships at night from the deadly U-boats. For many years after the war, the submarine nets which had been used to protect the entrance to the cape could be seen rusting away along the beach.

Early explorers found the areas of the Outer Banks of North Carolina abundant in fish and game. The Germans in both world wars also found a happy hunting ground here, but of quite another variety. Their prey was the unescorted merchant ship and oil tanker. Here where the coast of North America extends furthest eastward, they added their toll to the "Graveyard of the Atlantic."

As a six or seven-year-old in 1941-42, I recall the excited talk of the coastal residents as stories spread to Greenville and surrounding areas of ships burning and sinking off the coast.

As a teenager, I continued my interest in coastal Carolina by serving on the sailing staff of Camp Sea Gull, located near Oriental on the lower Neuse River. Later, in the 1960s and 70s, I frequented Ocracoke, Cape Lookout and the Pamlico Sound in my sailboat. Each visit made me appreciate more the Outer Bankers who, until a few years ago, earned their living from the sea.

Finally, my interest in U-boat activity off our coast during World War II was aroused while I attended a naval history symposium at Annapolis, Maryland, in the fall of 1987. Several German historians and even a former U-boat commander also attended. After over two years of research and interviews with participants, I have compiled this account of the early events of World War II along our coast.

Many friends and colleagues encouraged my efforts, particularly Jack Willis at Ocracoke, who used to keep an eye on my sailboat when I'd leave it for a few weeks. There was also a friend and retired hunting and fishing guide, Thurston Gaskill. Thurston was the Raleigh *News and Observer's* "Tar Heel of the Week" several years ago and is a lifelong resident of Ocracoke. I feel fortunate to have had the opportunity to hunt and fish with him for many years before he retired in 1988. George Coffman, an ardent student of World War II history, was another enthusiastic supporter of my research and this book.

Professionally, Jim (Speck) Caldwell, retired history professor at UNC-Chapel Hill; Jim Leutze, former Professor of War and Peace at UNC and now president of Hampton-Sydney College; and Bill Still, maritime history professor at East Carolina University, all kept encouraging me to complete this project. My gratitude goes to each and every one of them.

James T. Cheatham
Ocracoke, North Carolina
November 1989

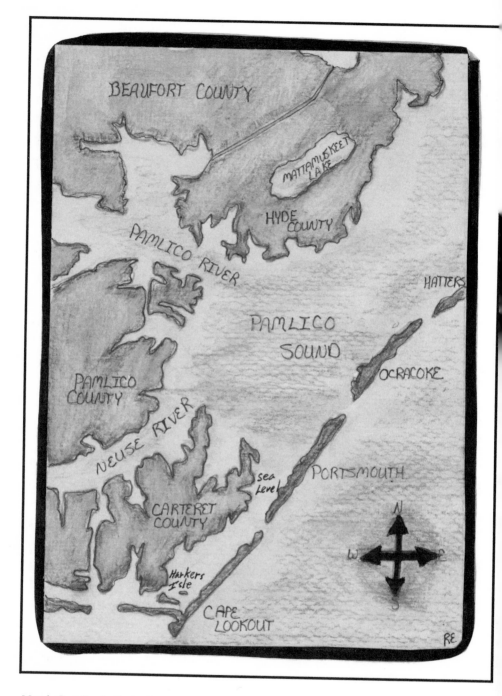

North Carolina's Outer Banks. Courtesy Re Johnston.

Chapter I

Winter, 1942

The new moon is black as ink.
Off Hatteras the tankers sink.
While sadly Roosevelt counts the score
Some fifty thousand tons. — Mohr

The verse quoted above is not some abstract poetry, but the actual war report of a German U-boat commander, Jochen Mohr (U-boat 124), written in early WWII to his superiors after sinking nine ships off the North Carolina coast.[1]

At a conservative estimate, from January, 1942, to the end of April, 1942, over 200 ships, totaling 1,150,675 tons, were destroyed on the Eastern Seaboard[2] (over 60 of these alone off the North Carolina coast). Only one U-boat was lost in the process.[3]

These easy pickings in the western Atlantic were referred to by the German captains with a borrowed American folk term as "the American turkey shoot."[4]

Sir Winston Churchill is credited with coining the term "U-boat" to apply to all German underwater craft and "submarine" to apply to similar vessels of Allied fleets. The reasoning behind this differentiation was that "'U-boats' are the dastardly villains who sink our ships, while 'submarines' are those gallant and noble craft which sink theirs."[5]

The war came quickly and disastrously to the whole Eastern Seaboard of the United States. Admiral Karl Donitz, head of German U-boat Command, realized early on that the United States was not prepared to combat the U-boat and seized the opportunity to strike American shipping within one month after Pearl Harbor.[6]

This was a welcome respite for the Germans from submarine warfare in the eastern Atlantic because the British had begun, through the Convoy System, air attacks, radar and ASDIC (sonar—a device which relied on reflection of sound impulses off submerged objects) to make inroads against the U-boats.

In March, 1941, Germany had lost three of its top U-boat aces: Gunther Prien, Joachim Schepke and Otto Kretschmer. In the fall and winter of 1941, the turning point was becoming apparent in all the theaters of the war. Before Moscow, the troops of the Wehrmacht—only a few weeks after the battle of encirclement at Kiev—were brought to a standstill for the first time. In North Africa the British troops went on the offensive.[7] The United States during this time was providing supplies for the Soviet Union and England and in September, 1941, became involved in escorting convoys. However, she was not formally at war until December 7, 1941, when Japan bombed Pearl Harbor and Germany declared war.

But while she quickly assembled fighting forces in the Pacific and in Europe after Pearl Harbor, the U.S. failed to adequately protect her own East Coast waters.

Chapter II

What the Germans Found

Surfacing within a mile offshore after sunset, the U-boat commanders could see—through binoculars—people walking around porches of homes close to the water.[8] They saw sleepy little fishing villages and resort towns with lights blazing. Even the buoys and lighthouses were in full operation, as well as radio stations to provide navigation assistance.

When asked several years ago if he had ever been to Long Island, former German U-boat Captain Klaus Friedland stated, "No, but I have seen it." And so he had—from a periscope of a German submarine, no less, in early World War II.[9]

Wolfgang Frank, author of *The Seawolves,* describes the happy conditions that the U-boat commanders found:

> There was still no evidence that the Americans were switching over to wartime conditions. After two months of war their ships were still sailing independently, their Captains stopped torpedoed ships and asked for information over the loud hailer; should a ship be hit but remain capable of steaming the Cap-

tain never bothered to zig zag or vary his speed so as to impede the U-boat in dealing with the coup de grace and they had no idea of security. They chatted about everything under the sun over the 600 meter wave band and as if that were not enough, the coastal defense stations sent out over the air a regular program of information, giving details of rescue work in progress, of where and when aircraft would be patrolling and the schedules of anti-submarine vessels.

Night surface attacks were preferred by the Germans for several reasons: (a) visibility was low, (b) the subs could make better speed on the surface, i.e., 17-19 knots as opposed to 7 underwater, (c) deck guns could be used on the surface, which helped to conserve torpedoes and, (d) the shallow coastal waters were more dangerous if the subs were submerged.

During the day the U-boats would lie on the sandy bottom. In fact, in some instances while doing so in shipping lanes, there would be a concern that ships passing overhead might hit the conning tower of the sub. Coastal buoys had not yet been extinguished, and these were used by the U-boats to silhouette the passing ships.[10]

In 1939 Admiral Donitz issued instruction No. 154 to his German submarine commanders:

> Rescue no one and take no one with you. Have no care for the ship's boats. Weather conditions and the proximity of land are of no account. Care only for your own boat and strive to achieve the next success as soon as possible. We must be hard in this war. The enemy started this war in order to destroy us; therefore nothing else matters.

The early months of action off the U.S. East Coast did not result in mass killings of ships' crews as one might have expected. Many torpedoed seamen lived to sail again in other merchant ships. Factors which led to this result were the facts that most ships sunk were traveling alone and the Germans, in an effort to conserve torpedoes, usually fired one torpedo, waited for the crew to disembark and then used their deck guns for the *coup de grace*. Moreover, the warmer Gulf Stream waters and the close proximity to land aided in successful rescue efforts.

Conversely, the American submarines operating in the far Pacific customarily fired at least three torpedoes at each ship. Only one U-boat captain was ever convicted of deliberately killing survivors in the water (Eck of U-852).

Despite many rumors of saboteurs being put ashore along the East Coast by U-boats, only two accounts were documented as accurate: one on Long Island sound and the other in Florida (near Ponte Vedra). Both resulted in arrest of the spies.[11]

U-123, seen above during her commissioning on May 30, 1940, was the first U-boat in coastal North Carolina waters. She sank nine ships for a total of 52,586 tons. Courtesy U.S. Naval Institute.

Left, Admiral Karl Donitz, head of German U-Boat Command, is credited with instituting the "American Turkey Shoot" in the winter of 1942. Courtesy U.S. Naval Institute.

Below left, Admiral Adolphus E. Andrews, who headed the navy's "Eastern Sea Frontier" from Canada to Florida and who felt the brunt of the first U-boat attacks along the East Coast. Courtesy U.S. Naval Institute.

Below right, Admiral Ernest J. King, commander-in-chief of the U.S. Fleet, who stubbornly refused to heed the advice of his British counterparts and institute convoys on the East Coast. Courtesy U.S. Naval Institute.

Jack Willis, Ocracoke native who witnessed the U-boat attacks before joining the navy. Courtesy Gan Photography.

Thurston Gaskill, Ocracoke hunting and fishing guide who witnessed U-boat attacks in WWII. Courtesy Ann Ehringhaus.

SS Bryon T. Benson *(tanker) burning off Cape Hatteras after being torpedoed by U-552 on April 5, 1943.* Courtesy U.S. Naval Institute.

German submarine U-85 in port during 1941. She was sunk off Nags Head on April 14, 1942. Courtesy U.S. Naval Institute.

A Coast Guardsman views the mast of a sunken vessel near the east coast of the United States early in WWII. Courtesy U.S. Naval Institute.

SS Dixie Arrow *(tanker) burning and sinking after being torpedoed by a German submarine off Cape Hatteras on March 26, 1942.* Courtesy U.S. Naval Institute.

Sinking of the SS Wyoming *early in WWII.* Courtesy U.S. Naval Institute.

USCGC Duane (WPG-33) *explodes a depth charge while hunting U-boats in the Atlantic in WWII.* Courtesy U.S. Naval Institute.

21

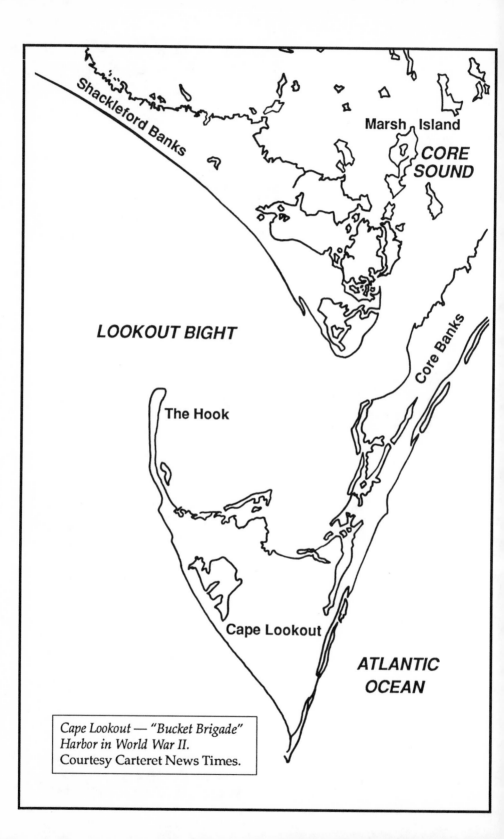

Shackleford Banks

Marsh Island

CORE SOUND

LOOKOUT BIGHT

Core Banks

The Hook

Cape Lookout

ATLANTIC OCEAN

Cape Lookout — "Bucket Brigade"
Harbor in World War II.
Courtesy Carteret News Times.

Chapter III

The Background—
U.S. Unpreparedness

In order to more fully understand the unpreparedness of the U.S. Atlantic Fleet during the early part of 1942, one must look at the background leading up to the Americans' entry into the war. Britain had been fighting the Germans for three years, and in 1940 the U.S. exchanged over fifty World War I destroyers, previously mothballed at the Philadelphia Navy Yard, for British bases in the West Indies and British Guiana. Forty-four of the four stackers were turned over to Britain and six were delivered to Canada.[12] On March 11, 1941, Congress passed the Lend-Lease Bill, which turned out to be one of the turning points of World War II. Under its terms Britain was to receive billions of dollars' worth of American equipment by June 30, 1942. Winston Churchill, whose country was then feeling the economic crunch of fighting a prolonged war, expressed his relief with his customary eloquence:

> The words and acts of the President and the people of the United States come to us like a draft of life and they tell us by an ocean born trumpet call that we are no longer alone.

Beginning in the early part of 1941, the British began to understand how to combat the German U-boat menace. Radar had then become operational, allowing ships and planes to locate German U-boats at night on the surface. Another big factor was the interception of German U-boat radio messages with radio detection finders. Also, between World War I and World War II, the British had developed an ASDIC, a type of sonar device carried under the hulls of ships that would send out a sound which, when it struck an underwater object, would give a "ping" back to the sender. It became a dreaded sound feared by U-boats throughout the rest of the war. The ASDIC (British name for its "Allied Submarine Detection Investigation Committee") was known in the United States as sonar.[13]

The British had also learned to use airplanes to their great advantage, including the flying boat which carried bombs and depth chargers and bristled with machine guns and was dubbed "The Flying Porcupine" by the Germans. Also, they had the ancient-looking biplane "Swordfish" which laid mines, dropped flares and attacked submarines and surface raiders with torpedoes. In addition, the British had catapult-equipped merchant ships which carried hurricane fighters that could not return to the deck once they were launched.[14]

However, the single most successful weapon against the U-boat—the convoy system—had been utilized in WWI and developed further in 1940 and 1941 by the British. By carefully analyzing the sinkings of their merchant ships, the British had developed a theory that if a wolfpack attacked a convoy of twenty ships and sank ten, it did not follow that the same wolfpack attacking a convoy of seventy ships would sink thirty-five. It would, in fact, probably sink no more than ten, which obviously called for larger convoys.

When the war was over, Admiral Donitz wrote, "The

German submarine campaign was wrecked by the introduction of the convoy system."[15]

Because the merchant ship presented the biggest target from bow to stern, the convoy's vessels were deployed only five deep, thereby minimizing the number exposed to flank attack. Oil tankers, troop transports, ammunition ships and vessels loaded with tanks, guns and other vital material were placed inside the formation. Ships were spread over an eighteen-mile-wide space with escorts circling the convoy at a range of about 5,000 yards. The convoy commodore was usually responsible for the merchant vessels and saw to it that they maintained their positions. The escort commander, under U-boat attack, took charge of the entire convoy, issuing orders to the convoy commodore even when outranked.[16]

At the beginning of 1942, the Germans had ninety-one submarines operational. Twenty-three were in the Mediterranean under orders from Hitler to attack Allied ships supplying British forces in the Egyptian desert. Six U-boats were positioned west of Gibraltar, and four were hovering off Norway. Of those remaining, over sixty percent were in dry dock for repairs. Thus, only twenty-two U-boats were active in the Atlantic, and approximately half of these were traveling to or from the combat zones.[17]

Admiral Donitz sent five U-boats into American waters in January of 1942 under the code name "Drum Roll" or "Beat of the Kettledrums." Donitz had proposed that twelve boats be sent to the American East Coast waters because he had seen that this was the Allies' most vulnerable point. However, Hitler rejected his proposal and declared that the Mediterranean was to remain the primary target area for U-boats. Nevertheless, Donitz's action had a devastating effect, and he later sent more U-boats.[18]

Between the 12th and the 31st of January, 1942, forty ships

were sunk in the North Atlantic. Of these, thirty-one, all sailing independently, had been twenty-six degrees west longitude, mostly off the American seaboard. In February, the number rose to fifty ships sunk in American waters out of a total of sixty-nine in the North Atlantic. March saw seventy-four ships lost in the same area. There was a slight drop in April to sixty-one.[19]

In July of 1942 came the introduction of the widespread convoy system from the Gulf of Mexico to Canada. The result was a dramatic change to almost total immunity in the areas where previously the sea had been littered with burning and sinking ships. The British, in 1917, were on the brink of total defeat when they introduced the convoy system and at once stopped the German sinkings. In spite of this example before them and further lessons passed on to them from experience in the Second World War by the British, the American naval authorities still held to doctrines and methods whose falsity had been starkly exposed.

The ultimate responsibility for the defense of shipping in American waters belonged to the commander-in-chief of the U.S. Atlantic Fleet, Admiral Ernest J. King (Annapolis, Class of 1901). Soon after the outbreak of war, King was elevated to commander-in-chief, U.S. Fleet, while the post of commander-in-chief, Atlantic Fleet, fell to Admiral R.E. Ingersoll.[20]

The new U-boat offensive took Americans by surprise, yet they did almost nothing to minimize its effect. Every day thousands of tons of irreplaceable cargo sailed unescorted up and down the coast. No instructions were given to captains as to what to do in the event of a U-boat attack. None of the planes that could fly far out to sea were on hand to do so, and few American pilots knew how to deal effectively with the U-boat if they spotted one.[21]

Worse, perhaps, the American ships were conspicuous and careless. Their personnel were both inexperienced and gullible. Ships' crews talked to each other on their radios, providing vital information to the lurking U-boats. One submarine commander, spying a freighter in the light of a tanker the U-boat had just set ablaze, signaled, "You're standing into danger. Direct your course to pass close to me." The freighter immediately obeyed and was torpedoed and sunk, losing twenty men.[22] Ashore, cities resisted the blackout orders.

The type of U-boat being used by the Germans at that time (type 1X-B or C) had such a short range that they were barely able to arrive at the East Coast and return home safely with enough fuel. In fact, they had to utilize water tanks and compartments to store extra fuel.[23] When torpedoes were in short supply, they resolved to use their deck guns to shell unprotected and hapless merchant vessels.

Naval authorities often were as perverse as the tourists, to the despair of the British, who after more than two years of painful trial and error in what one American admiral aptly described as the "laboratory of war," had virtually driven the U-boats from their coast.

The U.S. resisted all manner of British advice including, but not limited to, the tried and true Convoy System. The Americans contended that they lacked enough ships for proper escorts and that most of their ships were already in the North Atlantic for the run from Halifax to Iceland, the remainder being on duty in the Pacific.

In spite of World War I conclusions that the convoy system was the best and further assurances from the British that this was the major deterrent to the submarine war, Admiral King mistakenly believed the same methods of protection and similar escort forces would be necessary for coastal convoys as those crossing the ocean. However, U-boat "wolfpack" tactics could not be brought into play close to an enemy coast where reinforcements on the surface and in the air could quickly be summoned to the scene of a convoy being beset.[24]

Meanwhile, so totally unprotected were the merchant ships steaming independently within sight of the eastern shore of the United States that U-boats were able to pick them off one by one and even to surface and sink them by gunfire. Had only the meager forces available been used to escort convoys, however inadequately, experience elsewhere shows that the U-boats' success would have been much lessened.

Admiral King decided early in 1942 that until more escorts became available, a convoy system would have to wait. Perhaps this was a flawed decision because a force of destroyers of the U.S. Atlantic Fleet was available.

The naval command in charge of the area where the U-boats were making havoc was called "The Eastern Sea Frontier," extending from the Canadian border as far south as Florida. It was commanded by Vice Admiral Adolphus E. Andrews, King's classmate at Annapolis. The responsibility for these first U-boat attacks fell on Andrews.

In the face of violent newspaper agitation that something be done, Admiral Andrews asked for fifteen of the fleet destroyers in February. He got seven. These were sent out on patrol, rather than utilized in convoys. The patrols proved to be futile. Racing from one spot to another where U-boats had been located, they never succeeded in gaining contact with any of them. Naval historian Samuel Eliot Morison commented on the preparedness of the U.S. Navy:

> No scientific method of search to regain sound contact with a submarine had been worked out. U.S. destroyers were then so ill-fitted for search and so im-

perfectly trained for attack that to use them as roving patrol was worse than useless. It resulted only in the loss of one of the destroyers—USS Jacob Jones—torpedoed on 28 February. [1942].

According to the U.S. Fleet anti-submarine summary produced in July of 1945, the anti-submarine forces available to Americans in the North Atlantic in January, 1942, comprised 173 surface craft and 268 aircraft. By April of 1942, the number of surface craft was the same but the number of aircraft had risen to 589.

In the middle of May, 1942, when shipping losses were reaching intolerable proportions, the convoy was at last instituted on the United States East Coast with the average convoy being made up of about twenty-one ships and five or more escorts. Admiral King's contention that convoys could not be instituted in January of 1942, on account of shortage of escorts, cannot, based on the figures above, be accepted.[25]

It is probable that a change of heart took place in American naval circles in the late spring of 1942 as a result of the complete failure of their "offensive" methods. An example of this change is contained in a message to Admiral King from General George Marshall, Chief of Staff of the United States Army, who was deeply concerned with the heavy losses of army transports:

> We are well aware of the limited number of escort craft available, but has every conceivable means been brought to bear on this situation? I am fearful that another month or two will so cripple our means of transport that we will be unable to bring sufficient men and planes to bear against the enemy in critical theatres to exercise a determining influence on the war.

In his reply, King announced his views with all the fervor of a convert. "Escort," he said, "is not just one way of handling the submarine menace; it is the only way that gives any promise of success."[26] How different from this reply is that given by King to Admiral Pound, British First Sea Lord in March, 1942, when he stated that "Inadequately escorted convoys were worse than none."

The Americans tried riding their ships close to shore. This tactic only served to increase the density of the traffic stream and actually aided the U-boats. In April, shipping was restricted to moving only in daylight, anchoring for the night in Chesapeake Bay or Delaware Bay or in protected anchorages such as Cape Lookout. By this system, known as the "Bucket Brigade," the trip from Jacksonville to New York was made in four daylight runs.

Cape Lookout, a natural harbor, served the "Bucket Brigade" in April and May of 1942 as the stopping-over place between Charleston and the Chesapeake Bay. Submarine nets were placed across its entrance to keep the U-boats from slipping in at night to torpedo the anchored ships.

In spite of this tactic, shipping losses mounted steeply. U-boat commanders enjoyed coastal patrol because the pursuit required was less rigorous than that required with escorted convoys in the gales and fogs of the North Atlantic.

In late May the convoy system was put into place along the coast. The result is best given in Admiral Donitz's own words:

> At the end of April, the heavy sinkings off the east coast of America suddenly ceased. As this was a full moon period I hoped that the dark nights to follow would restore the situation and that the sinkings would regain their previous high level. Instead there

was a steady increase in signals from the U-boats, reporting no shipping sighted....

In light of unfavorable conditions off the coast of America and favorable conditions in the Caribbean, U-boat command at once transferred six boats from the former area to the latter and four other U-boats on the way to American waters from the Biscay ports were sent to the Caribbean.

Thus, the simple convoy system had diminished this blight on U.S. shipping. This was a remarkable vindication of the convoy system; however, so long as the system was not extended to the Gulf of Mexico and the Caribbean, U-boats sank over 250,000 tons (more than half of which were tankers) in the Gulf of Mexico alone. Another thirty-eight (more than 200,000 tons) were sent to the bottom in the Caribbean area.[27]

Some historians have speculated that the U-boats' successes in early 1942 off the North American coast were due to the U-tankers or "milch-cows." These were large, clumsy boats of nearly 1,700 tons without offensive capability but which carried quantities of stores and spare parts and 700 tons of diesel fuel for other boats. However, these were not even available at the time, their first sailing being on April 21, 1942. U-tankers were used in the Caribbean and Gulf of Mexico to great success but were not available during the East Coast "turkey shoot" in early 1942.[28]

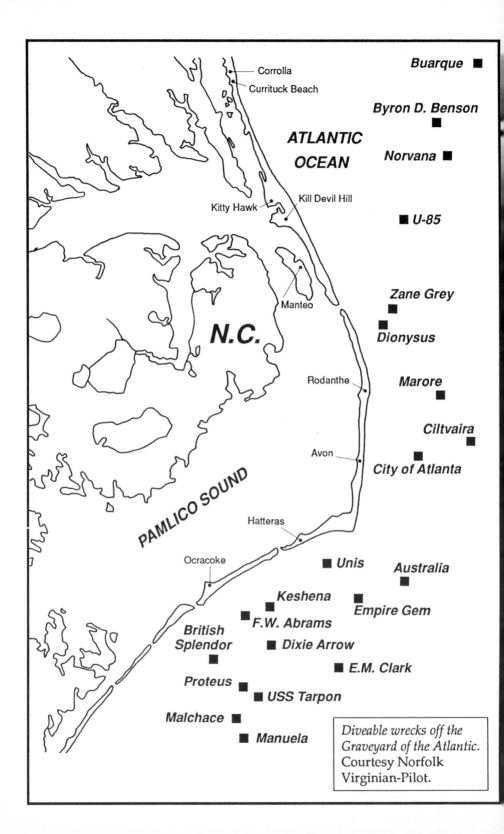

Diveable wrecks off the Graveyard of the Atlantic. Courtesy Norfolk Virginian-Pilot.

Chapter IV

Admiral King's Defense

Admiral King had two explanations for American unpreparedness in the face of the coastal submarine menace in early 1942. Available anti-submarine craft, he said, were fully committed to operations in the North Atlantic. He added that during the neutrality period of 1941, the U.S. had reinforced British convoy escorts and special escorts had to be provided for troop movements by sea and were also needed to furnish anti-submarine protection for our major combatant ships. Available aircraft were inadequate in numbers and deficient in anti-submarine weapons and devices. In many cases their personnel were untrained for submarine hunting.[29]

The Navy Department, according to King in his autobiography, had not been unaware of the situation the United States was getting into as the war approached. King tried to put the blame on Roosevelt. In his book he cites Admiral Harold Stark's unsuccessful efforts, early in 1941, to obtain approval for the construction of seagoing craft 250 to 300 feet in length and with a speed of 25 knots. King implies that Stark could not get presidential approval for these craft because Roosevelt was in favor of small patrol craft to counter the U-boat. King also attempts to blame "Operation Sledgehammer." This was the code name for the projected 1942 landing in Europe which, as we know, did not materialize and would have required the construction of a very large number of landing craft.

Although the army offered to provide aircraft for coastal patrolling, it preferred to follow the British practice, i.e., that all planes operating from shore bases would remain under an army air force coastal command. The navy argued that singleness of command was essential in anti-submarine operations.

Thus for two or three months while the sinkings continued, King argued with the air force about who was to command the land planes that had been requested. King contended that the Army Air Corps remained adamant in its refusal to assist the navy in the manner requested. This attitude was conveyed to King by the Assistant Secretary of the Navy for Air in a memorandum dated April 10, 1942, in which he stated that a meeting would be held with the president as soon as General Marshall returned from a visit to England.

Admiral King could not accept with equanimity statements in the British press that most of the convoy escorting was being done by British and Canadian ships and that the United States Navy was not helping out as much as it could and should. Such opinions led to a confrontation with Admiral Sir Andrew Cunningham, then head of the British Admiralty Delegation in Washington, in which King pointed out that "although the British had been managing world affairs for some 300 years, the United States Navy now had something to say about war at sea...."

Chapter V

Experiences of the Coastal Residents

Natives of the Outer Banks islands of North Carolina actually saw the war firsthand much more graphically than the Pacific Coast Americans who were involved only in the early fears of a Japanese invasion or air raid.

Paul Tyndall, recently a member of the N.C. House of Representatives from the 4th District, remembers well the early months of World War II on Harker's Island, a small island between Beaufort, North Carolina, and Cape Lookout.[30] He was the principal of the local school at Harker's Island. The residents of the island at that time consisted of many families who had moved over from an old whaling village at Cape Lookout called "Diamond City" after the hurricane of 1899. The island was isolated. It had no telephones, and the first bridge connecting it with the mainland was still being built.

Soon after the war started, passes were required for citizens to go over on the Outer Banks to fish. Tyndall and other coastal residents remember seeing many ducks and loons washed ashore, covered in oil from tankers that were sunk off the coast. At night the windows would occasionally be blown out by explosions of ships offshore.

In this atmosphere rumors started early about German spies and the possibility of signals from shore being given to U-boats. At Tyndall's school there was a teacher of German descent who was immediately suspected of being a spy and even followed by well-intentioned natives who suspected him of foul play. When he began to leave his home early in the morning and cross over to the mainland, the citizens immediately suspected he was rendezvousing with the enemy. As it turned out, he was only going to get milk for his children. By the end of the school year, he was forced to leave the island and seek employment elsewhere.

One day the principal noticed that many of the boys in school who usually came barefooted were wearing new Florsheim shoes. Investigation revealed that these had washed up on the Outer Banks from a merchant ship that was sunk by a U-boat. Fishermen had quickly commandeered these shoes, and their children wore them proudly.

During the spring of 1942, Tyndall's wife had to be transported to the Morehead City Hospital with a serious case of appendicitis. While she was a patient there, Tyndall visited the hospital daily and saw the many burn victims being treated. These victims were seamen who had been rescued off the coast from burning tankers. He assisted the nursing staff in caring for these patients because they were shorthanded at the time and the hospital was overflowing. The public was not made aware of this care for U-boat victims for fear of panic along the coast.

By that time, all houses were required to have blackout curtains at night, and cars could not drive with regular headlights. Owners had to have them painted so that only a small amount of light—just enough to drive by—would be emitted.

Farther up the coast at Ocracoke Island, Jack Willis, who

was then in his late teens and later served in the navy, remembers seeing as many as four or five ships burning at one time off the coast at night. Both he and long-time native, Thurston Gaskill, adamantly refute the rumor that native fishermen assisted German submarines off the coast.[31] In fact, investigation through the German Military Historical Research office has proved their contentions correct. Captain Werner Rahn, a German historian, in an interview in September, 1987, emphatically stated that he had read all the U-boat logs concerning East Coast activity. He said that there was absolutely no evidence of islanders selling supplies to U-boats. He said that he did not believe such help was given either on the East Coast or in the Caribbean area later on.[32]

On the sound near Salter Path, North Carolina, a small fishing village west of Atlantic Beach, lived Mrs. Alice Hoffman, whose niece married Theodore Roosevelt, Jr. She had purchased approximately a nine-mile portion of Bogue Banks in the early 1900s. Her name, of German origin, spurred many rumors that she was aiding the enemy. One such rumor had Mrs. Hoffman refueling submarines from the dock of her home. Since the water was only a few feet deep in the sound, even the author, who was about six years old then, could figure out that this was impossible. In fact, he remembers visiting Mrs. Hoffman with his mother about that time. There were no paved roads then in the area, only well-marked dirt paths. After the war, the author, with his uncle, visited Salter Path (still accessible only by boat or a dirt road) and talked to fishing families who were quick to tell of windows being blown out by exploding ships just off the coast, much debris and oil on the beach, and suspicious persons seen about during the spring of 1942.

None of their spy stories were ever proven true. The F.B.I., between January 1942 and May 15, 1943, investigated over 500 reports of refueling enemy subs on our shores, signaling to them and the like; but "every report...was a false alarm."[33]

Chapter VI

The Bedfordshire Incident

Alarmed by the large number of ships being sunk off the eastern coast of the United States, the British government in February, 1942, at the request of the United States, agreed to lend the United States Navy twenty-four anti-submarine corvettes. These ships were about half the size of a World War II type destroyer. They were 170 feet long, with a crew of four officers and thirty-three enlisted men. Their armament consisted of a four-inch, quick-fire deck gun and a 303-caliber Lewis machine gun. They also carried approximately 100 depth charges and sonar.

It seems ironic that only two years after the United States had given, through its lend-lease program, fifty destroyers to the English, the English would have to turn around and give us ships to combat our submarine menace.

Among the twenty-four coal-burning corvettes leaving England in early March was the HMS *Bedfordshire*.[34] The ships traveled through the North Atlantic to Newfoundland, then to Halifax, Nova Scotia and New York. At least one ship was lost during the winter gales on this trip. The others arrived in New York much in need of repairs.

Among the officers on board the *Bedfordshire* was Sub-

Lieutenant Thomas Cunningham. The *Bedfordshire* spent April and part of May patrolling off the North Carolina coast between Morehead City and Norfolk, with Morehead City as its home port. Because these ships were coal-burning, they required regular refueling.

In early May, Aycock Brown, assigned to the office of Naval Intelligence, visited the ship to obtain British flags to use in burial of Englishmen at Cape Hatteras who had lost their lives in ship sinkings. Sub-Lieutenant Cunningham was the officer who procured these flags for Brown. The *Bedfordshire* then refueled at Morehead City and left to check out a submarine sighting report. As it turned out, a German submarine (U-352) had been sunk near Cape Lookout by the Coast Guard cutter *Icarus*. As a result, the *Bedfordshire* stayed in that area for a day or so before proceeding on its patrol duty.

On the night of May 11, U-boat 558, captained by Gunther Krech, was cruising between Cape Hatteras and Cape Lookout. Its mission to date had been uneventful, and the captain was beginning to wonder if he would have as successful a cruise on the American coast as his counterparts. Suddenly, the noises of a ship's screw were heard on the submarine's listening device, and a lookout saw the HMS *Bedfordshire*.

Visibility was low. Because of the faster speed at which submarines can move on the surface, U-558 made its attack on the surface. After missing with its first torpedo, the submarine's second torpedo hit the *Bedfordshire* squarely amid ships, catapulting the ship into the air and sinking it almost immediately. No one survived this sinking to explain how the "hunter was killed by the hunted." We can only speculate that our British friends had become too complacent in their efforts to assist their allies.

The U.S. Navy, to which the British ships were attached,

was not very diligent in keeping track of these patrol craft, as evidenced by the fact that the navy was not aware of what had happened to the HMS *Bedfordshire* for several days.

On May 14th, while patrolling the shore at Ocracoke Island, North Carolina, a Coast Guardsman discovered the bodies of Sub-Lieutenant Thomas Cunningham and telegraphist Stanley Craig. Later two other bodies, unidentifiable, were recovered. These were removed to a small plot next to a local cemetery at Ocracoke Village and, with Coast Guard assistance and protestant graveyard services, they were given proper burial. Ironically, the flag used for Cunningham's funeral was one of the very ones given by him to Aycock Brown about ten days earlier.

In subsequent years, with the cooperation of the United States government and the citizens of Ocracoke Island, this small plot was deeded to the British government and is now an official English cemetery. It can be viewed today on Ocracoke Island. Permanent grave markers are present and a British flag flies continuously over the site to remind all who see it of the brave men who fought in World War II and died in defense of democracy. It is also a reminder of the close ties we in this country have to our mother country, England.

USS Pillsbury (DE-133) *capturing German sub U-505 near the end of WWII.* Courtesy U.S. Naval Institute.

Even sailboats were requisitioned by the navy to aid in patrol, search and rescue off the East Coast. Courtesy U.S. Naval Institute.

U-977, a 773-ton U-boat which belonged to the most numerous submarine class of the German navy. Courtesy U.S. Naval Institute.

A World War II convoy leaves New York Harbor headed for Europe. Courtesy U.S. Naval Institute.

Destroyer DD-130, USS Jacob Jones, *became a victim of U-boat attack by U-578 on the night of February 27, 1942, off the U.S. East Coast.* Courtesy U.S. Naval Institute.

A British coal-burning corvette similar to the HMS Bedfordshire, *which was sunk by a U-boat near Ocracoke on the night of May 11, 1942.* Courtesy U.S. Naval Institute.

Above, a British flag drapes the coffin of Sub-Lieutenant Thomas Cunningham during burial at Ocracoke in May, 1942. This was the same flag given to Aycock Brown a few days earlier by Cunningham. Courtesy National Park Service.

Graveyard services being conducted at Ocracoke in May, 1942, for four British seamen from the torpedoed HMS Bedfordshire. Courtesy National Park Service.

British cemetery on Ocracoke where four British sailors of the HMS Bedfordshire *are buried.* Courtesy Gan Photography.

45

Picturesque Ocracoke Harbor today. During WWII it was enlarged to accommodate the navy station's needs. Courtesy Gan Photography.

U.S. Coast Guard station in 1940 at Ocracoke, North Carolina.

J. Paul Tyndall, former representative from Onslow County to the N.C. General Assembly, and principal of Harker's Island School during WWII.

Seamen's retirement home at Sea Level, North Carolina. Courtesy Gan Photography.

ENGLAND'S CONVOY SYSTEM

A WINNING COMBINATION

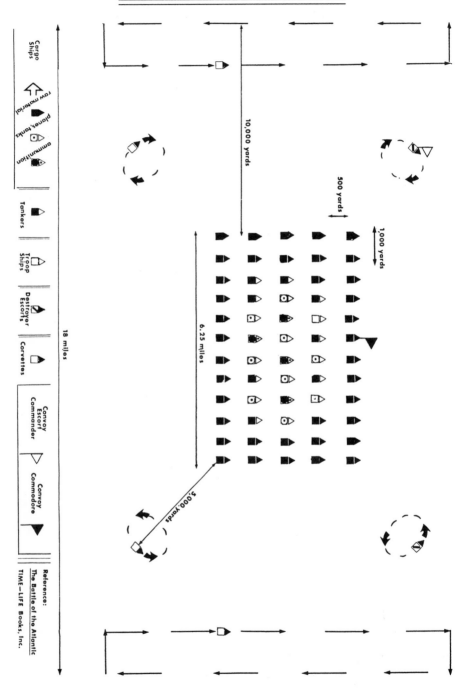

Chapter VII

Fate of the Torpedoed Ships' Crews

It wasn't until the fall of 1945 that the Fifth Naval District released the number of merchant seamen and guncrews lost off the coast by Axis submarines in World War II. In this district's waters, which extend halfway to Bermuda and include the shores of Maryland, Virginia and North Carolina down south to Onslow Bay, 843 men lost their lives.[35]

Today, standing on the shore at the north end of Ocracoke Island, watching the white caps lap over the Diamond Shoals, one can truly understand why this area has become known, along with the Banks of Newfoundland, as the "Graveyard of the Atlantic." World War II simply added its share to the vast cemetery of sunken ships.

Many crewmen survived to sail another day; many others were injured and treated at hospitals in Morehead City and Norfolk. The authorities, at the time, were fearful of civilian panic and did not disclose the numbers killed or injured.

The sinkings off North Carolina began on January 18, 1942, with the torpedoing of the tanker *Alan Jackson* off Hatteras. Twenty-two crewmen perished. Northbound tankers loaded with much needed fuel oil were a favorite target of the U-boats, and in the first year alone, thirty-five were attacked in the Fifth Naval District area.

Along the Virginia Capes, the enemy began to get bolder, laying mines in approaches to the Chesapeake Bay and occasionally surfacing within sight of bathers at Virginia Beach to finish off a hapless merchant vessel with shellfire.[36]

In February, the *Blink*, a small Norwegian freighter, was sunk off Hatteras. An Atlantic winter gale accounted for eight of the twenty-four who perished. They died after drifting in a lifeboat for three days. Six survived the ordeal.[37]

On March 11, the American freighter *Caribasca* was sunk near Ocracoke. Survivors were tossed about on life rafts all day until they used a metal can as a reflector to attract a passing steamship, *Norlindo*, bound for Baltimore; however, twenty-one of the crew were lost. One of those lost was James Gaskill from Ocracoke. The ship's nameplate is said by island residents to have floated through the Ocracoke inlet and washed ashore near where Gaskill lived. Marvin Howard found it and made a cross which can be seen today in the Methodist church located on the island. James Gaskill was the brother of Thurston Gaskill, who still resides on the island and witnessed many of the U-boat attacks offshore.[38]

A questionable sinking occurred March 14 when a torpedo pierced the American freighter *Liberator* near Diamond Shoals. She quickly sank but the question remains to this day why the Germans did not get the much larger and newer Esso tanker *Baltimore*, which was only a hundred yards ahead. Perhaps their aim was bad and they were reluctant to stay in the area to finish off the real prize.

On March 26, the tanker *Dixie Arrow* was sunk near Hatteras (see photograph). The captain, all deck officers and the radio operator were lost.[39]

By the end of March, some merchant ships carried deck guns and trained gunners to ward off surface attackers.

Despite this precaution, the American cargo passenger ship *City of New York* was sunk near Hatteras on March 27 with a loss of life of thirty-three out of a total of forty-one passengers, eighty-eight crewmen and nine gunners. Four lifeboats were used by the survivors, who were picked up by the USS *Roper*. One of these contained a pregnant passenger who gave birth to a baby boy during the cold March night. By luck, the ship's doctor was aboard this particular raft. Mother and baby survived with the baby being given the middle name Roper in honor of his rescuer.[40]

Burning oil was the greatest threat to tanker crews. In one incident off Hatteras, twenty-eight crew members of the British tanker *San Delfino* drifted into a burning oil slick and perished. Likewise, thirty-two survivors of the tanker *Atlas*, sunk near Cape Lookout, were taken to Morehead City for treatment of burns.

Once a ship's survivor managed to get to a lifeboat or raft, his ordeal was not always over, especially if he was a long way from the shore. Such was the case of crewman John Souza of the ship *Alcon Guide*, who drifted in the Atlantic for a month before he was rescued. Three of his companions were not so lucky and died aboard the raft.[41]

In 1976 a retirement home for aged mariners was moved from New York to Sea Level, North Carolina. Sea Level is located thirty miles north of Morehead City and Beaufort. Founded in 1801 by Captain Robert Richard Randall, a ship's master and revolutionary war hero, the home, Sailors' Snug Harbor, has become a haven for aged mariners.

With the guidance of his close associate, Alexander Hamilton, Randall arranged to bequeath his twenty-one-acre estate, located in what is now the heart of Greenwich Village, to a perpetual trust. The purpose of this trust was to provide a home for "aged, decrepit and worn out seamen." The trust still owns much of the estate today and collects rents on those New York properties. Built originally on Staten Island's Kill Van Kull in 1833, the first Sailors' Snug Harbor housed over 11,000 disabled and retired mariners.

The retirement home admits merchant seamen and women who are no longer able to pursue their seagoing careers and who meet a basic requirement of at least ten years of deep sea service. Among applicants who meet these criteria, admission is based solely on need.

Some seamen who were on ships torpedoed during WWII still reside in Snug Harbor and can recite stories of their experiences with the U-boats and subsequent rescue at sea. While this author was visiting there, an old sailor sitting in the lobby was overheard saying, "that young author believes all these stories they are telling him."

Conclusion

Had the United States listened early on to our British counterparts' advice to institute convoys on our East Coast, perhaps the Germans' East Coast "turkey shoot" would not have been such a success. Hitler's refusal to heed his U-boat commander's recommendation of sending twelve submarines in lieu of five to our East Coast in early 1942 probably saved the country an oil, sugar and coffee crisis. As it was, all three soon had to be rationed. At that time there were no pipelines to aid in the delivery of oil and gas from Texas and the Gulf Coast to the metropolitan cities on our northeast coast.

England's ability to stockpile war materials for pending operations against the Axis was curtailed. By June 20, 1942, a cross-channel invasion for 1943 to open a "second front" was ruled out. While all such postponements and setbacks cannot be directly linked to the success of the German U-boats off the American coast, Donitz's submarine offensive unquestionably restricted Allied operations. The U-boats were making their mark and the Americans "despaired of hunting the hornets all over the farm."[42]

Footnotes

1. Wolfgang Frank, *Seawolves—The Story of Germany's U-Boats at War* (London: Weidenfeld and Nicolson, 1955).

2. Douglas Bolting and others (eds.), *Seafarers, The U-Boats* (Alexandria, Virginia: Time-Life Books, 1979), hereinafter cited as *Seafarers, The U-Boats.*

3. David Stick, *Graveyard of the Atlantic* (Chapel Hill: The University of North Carolina Press, 1952).

> On the morning of April 14, 1942, the U.S. destroyer Roper caught the submarine U-85 surfaced off Nags Head, North Carolina, and sunk her with surface fire and depth charges.

4. *Seafarers, The U-Boats.*

5. Ernest J. King and Walter Whitehill, *A Naval Record* (New York: W.W. Norton & Co., 1952), hereinafter cited as *A Naval Record.*

6. Peter Padfield, *Donitz* (New York: Harper & Row, 1984).

> The results are described in Donitz's war diary; here is his note after the return of the first U-boat in the operation—called Paukenschlag (Beat of the Kettledrums):
>
>> The expectation of coming across much single-ship traffic, clumsy handling of ships, few and unpracticed sea and air patrols and defenses was so greatly fulfilled that the conditions have to be described as almost of peacetime standards. The single disposition of boats was, therefore, correct. The Commander found such an abundance of opportunities for attack in the sea area south of New York to Cape Hatteras that he could not possibly use them all. At times up to ten ships were in sight, sailing with lights on peacetime courses....

7. Lothar-Gunther Buchheim, *The Boat* (New York: Alfred Knoff, 1975).

8. Lecture by Klaus Friedland, former U-boat commander, at The

Eighth Annual Naval History Symposium—U.S. Naval Academy—Annapolis, Maryland, September 24, 1987, hereinafter cited as Klaus Friedland.

9. Klaus Friedland.

10. Peter Kemp, *Decision at Sea—The Convoy Escorts* (New York: Elsevier: Dutton, 1978), hereinafter cited as *Decision at Sea;* and Klaus Friedland.

11. Author's interview with professor Dr. Jurgen Rohwer, German historian, October 20, 1989, Annapolis, Maryland (notes in possession of author).

12. Barrie Pitt and others (eds.), *The Battle of the Atlantic—World War II* (Alexandria, Virginia: Time-Life Books, 1980), hereinafter cited as *The Battle of the Atlantic.*

13. *The Battle of the Atlantic.*

14. *Decision at Sea.*

15. *The Battle of the Atlantic.*

16. *The Battle of the Atlantic.*

17. *The Battle of the Atlantic.*

18. *The Battle of the Atlantic.*

19. Winston Churchill, *The Second World War,* Volume IV, (London: Cassell & Co., Ltd., 1951).

20. Donald Macintyre, *The Naval War Against Hitler* (New York: Charles Scribner's Sons, 1971), hereinafter cited as *Naval War Against Hitler.*

21. *The Battle of the Atlantic.*

22. *The Battle of the Atlantic.*

23. *Naval War Against Hitler.*

24. *Naval War Against Hitler.*

25. *Naval War Against Hitler.*

26. Samuel Eliot Morison, *The Two Ocean War* (Boston: Atlantic, Little, Brown, 1963); and *Naval War Against Hitler.*

27. *Naval War Against Hitler.*

28. Klaus Friedland.

29. *A Naval Record.*

30. Author's interview with Paul Tyndall, member of the N.C. House of Representatives from Onslow County, February 13, 1988 (notes in possession of author).

31. Author's interviews with Jack Willis, Ocracoke Island, December 20, 1987, and Thurston Gaskill, July 1986 (notes in possession of author).

32. Author's interview with Captain Werner Rahn, West German Navy (head, German Military Historical Research Office), September 25, 1987, Annapolis, Maryland (notes in possession of author).

33. Quote by J. Edgar Hoover, director, Federal Bureau of Investigation, *American Magazine*, October 1943, p. 110.

34. Information for this chapter drawn from two sources:
(1) L. Vanloan Narisawald, *In Some Foreign Field (The Story of Four British Graves on the Outer Banks)* (Winston-Salem, North Carolina: John F. Blair, publisher, 1972).
(2) Articles appearing in *The News and Observer*, published by The News and Observer Publishing Co., Raleigh, N.C.

35. Fifth Naval District Press Release, September 1945.

36. *Norfolk Virginian-Pilot*, September 16, 1945, hereinafter cited as *Virginian-Pilot.*

37. *Virginian-Pilot.*

38. Author's interview with Jack Willis, fall 1989, Ocracoke, N.C. (notes in possession of author).

39. *Virginian-Pilot.*

40. *Virginian-Pilot.*

41. *Virginian-Pilot.*

42. T.J. Belke, *Roll of the Drums,* Annapolis: U.S. Naval Institute Proceedings, April 1983.

> Note: The method of hunting U-boats by destroyers on random patrol, first tried in WWI, had caused President Woodrow Wilson to refer to it as "hunting the hornets all over the farm" (Elting E. Morrison, *Admiral Simms,* p. 361).

Appendix

List of Ships Lost off North Carolina from January through June, 1942

NAME	TYPE	DATE	PLACE
Allan Jackson	Tanker	Jan. 18, 1942	Cape Hatteras
Brazos	Cargo	Jan. 18, 1942	Cape Hatteras
Norvana	Cargo	Jan. 18, 1942	Cape Hatteras
City of Atlanta	Cargo	Jan. 19, 1942	Cape Hatteras
Ciltvaira	Tanker	Jan. 20, 1942	Gull Shoal
Empire Gem	Tanker	Jan. 23, 1942	Creeds Hill
Venore	Cargo	Jan. 23, 1942	Creeds Hill
York	Cargo	Jan. ?, 1942	Kill Devil Hills
Amerikalund	(?)	Feb. 2, 1942	Wash Woods
Victolite	Tanker	Feb. 10, 1942	Caffeys Inlet
Blink	Cargo	Feb. 11, 1942	Cape Hatteras
Buarque	Passenger	Feb. 15, 1942	Kill Devil Hills
Olympic	Tanker	Feb. 23, 1942	Kill Devil Hills
Norlavore	Cargo	Feb. 24, 1942	Cape Hatteras
Cassimir	Tanker	Feb. 26, 1942	Cape Fear
Marore	Cargo	Feb. 26, 1942	Gull Shoal
Raritan	Cargo	Feb. 28, 1942	Cape Fear
Anna R. Heidritter	Schooner	Mar. 1, 1942	Ocracoke
Arabutan	Cargo	Mar. 7, 1942	Cape Hatteras
Chester Sun	Tanker	Mar. 10, 1942	Big Kinnakeet
Caribsea	Cargo	Mar. 11, 1942	Cape Lookout
John D. Gill	Tanker	Mar. 12, 1942	Cape Fear
Ario	Tanker	Mar. 15, 1942	Cape Lookout
Ceiba	Cargo	Mar. 15, 1942	Nags Head
Resource	(?)	Mar. 15, 1942	Kill Devil Hills
Alcoa Guide	Cargo	Mar. 16, 1942	Cape Hatteras

NAME	TYPE	DATE	PLACE
Olean	Tanker	Mar. 16, 1942	Cape Lookout
Tenas	Barge	Mar. 17, 1942	Creeds Hill
Australia	Tanker	Mar. 17, 1942	Diamond Shoals
Papoose	Tanker	Mar. 18, 1942	Cape Lookout
W.E. Hutton	Tanker	Mar. 18, 1942	Bogue Inlet
E.M. Clark	Tanker	Mar. 18, 1942	Ocracoke
Liberator	Cargo	Mar. 19, 1942	Cape Hatteras
Kassandra Louloudis	Cargo	Mar. 19, 1942	Cape Hatteras
Teresa	Cargo	Mar. 21, 1942	Cape Hatteras
Naeco	Tanker	Mar. 23, 1942	Cape Lookout
Empire Steel	Tanker	Mar. 24, 1942	Wash Woods
Narraganset	Tanker	Mar. 25, 1942	Cape Hatteras
Dixie Arrow	Tanker	Mar. 26, 1942	Ocracoke
Carolyn	Cargo	Mar. 27, 1942	Nags Head
Equipoise	Cargo	Mar. 27, 1942	Caffeys Inlet
City of New York	Passenger	Mar. 29, 1942	Cape Hatteras
Malchase	Cargo	Mar. 29, 1942	Cape Lookout
Rio Blanco	Cargo	Apr. 1, 1942	Cape Hatteras
Otho	Cargo	Apr. 3, 1942	Cape Hatteras
Byron D. Benson	Tanker	Apr. 3, 1942	Caffeys Inlet
Ensis	Tanker	Apr. 4, 1942	Cape Hatteras
British Splendour	Tanker	Apr. 6, 1942	Cape Hatteras
Lancing	Tanker	Apr. 7, 1942	Cape Hatteras
Kollskegg	Tanker	Apr. 7, 1942	Cape Hatteras
San Delfino	Tanker	Apr. 9, 1942	Cape Hatteras
Atlas	Tanker	Apr. 9, 1942	Cape Lookout
Tamaulipas	Tanker	Apr. 10, 1942	Cape Lookout
Tennessee	Tanker	Apr. 11, 1942	Cape Lookout
U-85	German sub	Apr. 14, 1942	Nags Head
Empire Thrush	Cargo	Apr. 14, 1942	Cape Hatteras
Desert Light	Cargo	Apr. 16, 1942	Oregon Inlet
Empire Dryden	Cargo	Apr. 19, 1942	Oregon Inlet

NAME	TYPE	DATE	PLACE
Harpagon	Cargo	Apr. 19, 1942	Cape Hatteras
Agra	Tanker	Apr. 20, 1942	Cape Hatteras
Chenango	Cargo	Apr. 20, 1942	Kill Devil Hills
Bris	Cargo	Apr. 21, 1942	Cape Lookout
Ashkabad	Cargo	Apr. 29, 1942	Cape Lookout
Lady Drake	Cargo	May 5, 1942	Oregon Inlet
Senateur Duhamel	Trawler	May 6, 1942	Fort Macon
U-352	German sub	May 9, 1942	Cape Lookout
Bedfordshire	Trawler	May ?, 1942	Cape Lookout
West Notus	Cargo	June 1, 1942	Cape Hatteras
Manuela	Cargo	June 5, 1942	Cape Lookout
Pleasantville	Cargo	June 8, 1942	Cape Hatteras
F.W. Abrams	Tanker	June 10, 1942	Ocracoke
U.S.S.Y.P. 389	Antisub	June 19, 1942	Cape Hatteras
Ljubica Matkovic	Cargo	June 24, 1942	Core Bank
Nordal	Cargo	June 24, 1942	Ocracoke
William Rockefeller	Tanker	June 28, 1942	Cape Hatteras
City of Birmingham	Cargo	June 30, 1942	Cape Hatteras

Reprinted from David Stick, *Graveyard of the Atlantic,* Chapel Hill: University of North Carolina Press, Chapel Hill, North Carolina, 1952, by permission of the UNC Press.

Order Additional Copies of
The Atlantic Turkey Shoot

☒ **Postal orders:** Gan Productions, Rt. 9, Box 324A, Greenville, NC 27858.

Please send _____ copies of **The Atlantic Turkey Shoot** to:

Name _____

Address _____

_____

☐ Add my name to your mailing list so that I may receive more information on future books.

_____ Books @ $9.95   _____

Mailing Charges
    Please include **$2.00** for the first book and **75 cents**
    for each additional book. (Surface shipping may take
    three to four weeks.)
    ✈ Air mail: **$3.00** per book   _____

Sales Tax
    Please add 6% for NC sales tax if you
    are NC resident   _____

Total Due   ═══════════════

☐ My check is enclosed.

ML